86 DUMPLINGS
OF INSIGHT INTO CHINA

STORIES ABOUT CHINA, CHINA'S
PEOPLE AND THE CHINESE
WAY OF LIFE.

SALLY WATERS

Copyright © 2014 by Sally Waters.

Studio China
PO Box 5653
MANLY QLD 4179

http://www.studiochina.com.au

National Library of Australia Cataloguing-in-Publication entry

Creator: Waters, Sally, author.

Title: 86 dumplings of insight into China : stories about China, China's people and the Chinese way of life / Sally Waters.

Edition: 2nd edition.

ISBN: 9780646931975 (paperback)

Subjects: Chinese–Anecdotes.
China–Biography.
China–Social life and customs.
China–Description and travel.

Dewey Number: 951.0612

All rights reserved. Except as permitted under the Australian Copyright Act 1968, no part of this publication may be reproduced, stored in a retrieval system, communicated or transmitted in any form or by means, electronic, mechanical, photocopying, recording, or otherwise, without the prior written permission of the publisher. All inquiries should be made to the publisher at the above address.

Disclaimer: The material in this publication is of the nature of general comment only and does not represent individual advice. It is not intended to provide specific guidance for particular circumstances and should not be relied on as the basis for any decision to take action or not to take action on any matters which it covers.

Readers should obtain professional advice where appropriate, before making any such decision. To the maximum extent permitted by law, the author and publisher disclaim all responsibility and liability to any person, arising directly or indirectly from any person taking or not taking action based on the information in this publication.

Contents

Introduction 1

"Have you eaten yet?" 3

"Are you wearing enough?" 4

Open-hearted 5

A working life 6

China is vast and old 7

It gets complicated 8

They love Australia 9

Mixed marriages 10

Displays of physical affection 11

Clean feet 13

Aunties and Uncles 14

Animal zodiac 15

Your salary is public knowledge 16

Calcium in the Chinese diet 17

Cute babies 18

Never going thirsty 19

People and restaurants everywhere 21

The beauty of steam 22

Infrequent showering 23

Chinese people are not all short 25

100-day-old birthday 26

The fourth trimester 27

Central Kingdom 29

White is beauty 30

Chinese New Year.. 31

Having sons... 32

Daily visits to the fresh food market... 34

Active lives... 35

Little emperors.. 36

Good health... 38

Discretionary spending 39

Barbers on the street 40

Special names for relatives 41

Climbing mountains 43

"Cheers" means "scull".. 44

A kid's education 45

Pressure to settle down 46

What is the meaning of "good"?... 47

He or she.. 48

Raw noodles 49

Peanuts... 50

Chilli... 51

Daughter's choice of husband 52

Wedding Day 54

Ducks swimming on the pond 55

Eat slowly... 56

Living life by passing the days 57

Women hold up half the sky 58

Don't flip the fish!... 60

The red thread	61
"Deeds not Words"	62
Red packet	63
Pear superstition	64
Big home	65
Handing over money for nothing	66
Thanks for having a son	67
A tall nose	68
Students' pastimes	69
A spare patch	70
What is retirement for?	71
Money in the bank	72
The importance of prosperity	73
A flying kiss	74
Family finances	75
Birthday noodles	76
Prioritising	77
The story of Mulan	78
No sex education in China	79
The sounds of tropical Queensland	80
The sounds of the street	81
Big breakfast	82
Where are all the people?	84
Morbid fascination	85
Foreigners on TV	86
"Wang rhymes with tongue"	87

Babies crawling on the wedding bed 88

Feng shui 89

Super mum 90

Parents and children living apart 91

And husbands and wives, too 92

Simplified characters 93

Wrinkles 94

Dr Phil 95

Everybody gives way to everybody 96

Chinese Frére Jacques 97

Wade & Giles, tones and Cantonese 98

Conclusion: May the sampling continue 100

Acknowledgements 101

INTRODUCTION

One Christmas when I was growing up, my sister was given a book about China. It was a large, hardcover book and the big glossy photos inside really caught my attention. It gave me the impression that China was a country of beautiful misty mountains with small tea pavilions built atop, and mysterious women in colourful silk gowns. It seemed such a contrast to tropical Queensland, where I grew up.

I recently rediscovered this book. As I turned the pages and looked at the photos again, I found that, as an adult, my mind was drawn to different images. I suppose now that I am more politically aware, I find myself captivated by the photos towards the end of the book, taken in the late 1970s. Among others, there are photos of Mao Zedong's red guards dressed in dark Mao suits. The book was published in the early 1980s. As a girl, I hadn't comprehended any of the political meaning in these final pages.

Despite my fascination with the book, as a child I had no idea what a large influence China would have on my life. I was a girl, leafing through this glossy book. Meanwhile, my future husband was a boy living within the walls of a communist factory compound in the middle of China.

Skip forward about 30 years to now, and we are married and have three small children. I've lived in China on and off since 1997. We live in Brisbane, Australia now, and in spite of our fortunate life here, I often yearn for life in China, maybe even more often than my husband does.

At university in Australia, I studied a double major in Chinese, and I fell in love with the language. Through my teachers' stories, I started to see how Chinese people view the world. Their perspective was unique and refreshing to me. Since my very first Mandarin lesson, I have been a student of the Chinese way of life. And it has enriched my own life.

When I was at home caring for my babies, I started recording little stories in a notebook, whenever they came to me, about life in China. And here I share these stories with you. They are about my experiences of:

- life in China,
- how Chinese people view Australia,
- how Chinese people think and live, and
- being a wife, daughter-in-law and mother in a Chinese family.

I hope my first-hand observations as recorded here will offer insights into Chinese traditions and behaviours.

I want you to know that China is very diverse. There are many, many Chinese traditions, cultures and ways of life. China is a massive country, bigger in area than Australia, and it has so many people spread all over it. There are 56 different racial groups in the country, so there is much diversity. There are also hundreds of languages spoken across different regions. The observations that I share in this book about China and its people are just my experiences. There are different customs and traditions and foods and festivals all over China. It is likely, then, that others will have different observations and realities.

There are 86 dumplings (a lucky Chinese number, as you will see) of insight for you to digest in this book. Their order is mostly organic – they are roughly in the order that I jotted them down in my notebook. Some ideas only take a couple of sentences to explain, and others take pages. You can read it front to back, or dive in wherever you like.

I hope they prove useful and interesting to you, whether you are visiting or moving to China, or simply an armchair traveller.

"Have you eaten yet?"

What do we normally say to each other in English when we greet someone at our house, or when we bump into them on the street? We probably say: "Hi, how are you?" or "What's been happening?" or "How have you been?"

There is something we are neglecting to ask which is somewhat more important, isn't there? Think like a Chinese person for a moment. What is life all about for most Chinese people? Yes, that's right: food. You've forgotten to ask: "Have you eaten?" This is actually a pretty important matter. In China, everything relates to your last meal or your next meal. I think that it's actually a lovely, caring and kind thing to ask. No one is ever very good if they are hungry after all, are they? So next time you meet your friend, do the Chinese thing and check that they've had their lunch.

It is also okay to say to someone, "Where are you going?" – which might sound a bit nosey in English. If you really don't want to tell them where you are going, you can always reply, "out". They should get the message.

"ARE YOU WEARING ENOUGH?"

Your Chinese friends are almost always likely to comment on what you are wearing. They may observe that you're wearing too much (usually in winter, when you've worn your puffy coat but it's actually not that cold for some reason), or that you are not wearing enough when you are dressed just right. The Chinese err on the side of overdressing. Their concern for what you are wearing can be pretty irritating, but you can just remind yourself that they are simply showing care and concern for your well-being. And who could begrudge them that?

OPEN-HEARTED

To us, an open heart means major cardiac surgery. But to the Chinese, to be open-hearted means that you are happy. And a pistachio is called the open-heart nut in Chinese – because it looks just like one. Don't you agree that having an open heart is a great way to express happiness? I think it implies a lightness of spirit and openness to the wonder in the world.

A WORKING LIFE

Billions of Chinese people are working their lives away instead of actually living life, just as most people in the developed world do. In China, life is much more about survival and less about comfort and enjoyment. More than 50% of Chinese people still live and work in rural settings.

Most people living in China's cities tend to live lives similar to ours in terms of material wealth. But these relatively affluent city-dwellers do not make up the majority of people in China.

CHINA IS VAST AND OLD

Chinese civilisation is one of the oldest in the world. I've gained an appreciation of the vastness of China and of the diversity and richness of Chinese culture from my undergraduate studies of Chinese culture, and from hours and hours spent observing people in China.

Now that I'm a member of a Chinese family, I like to think that I've also gained some understanding of China's recent political events, and how they have impacted on its people and their connection to traditional ways. But I'm often reminded by my father-in-law that I'm only just scraping the surface.

It gets complicated

The traditions, customs, rituals and intricacies of the Chinese language, which are used to convey respect and demonstrate your understanding, are thick and complicated. Chinese people are often very indirect communicators, and they value this custom. I often see Chinese people continually plotting to convey themselves in a certain light.

I tend to be a very direct person, and I am learning that this won't always get me what I want when relating to Chinese people. I normally endear myself to people by being upfront and friendly, and while Chinese people will certainly be very friendly, they are rarely upfront. You may be wrong to assume that a friendly smile means they are on your side.

I recently heard a former Australian Ambassador to China comment on the radio that, despite years and years of political and cultural engagement, the challenges in the relationship between China and Australia are still deeply entrenched. The differences between our views of the world are great. Even though we continue to engage with our Chinese counterparts in embassies in Canberra and Beijing, in trade offices in Shanghai and Sydney, in joint-venture mining projects and in many other ways, such as cultural partnerships, the same cultural frictions appear in each new encounter. Long-running relationships can be rich and rewarding, but I am fairly confident they are never completely straightforward.

THEY LOVE AUSTRALIA

What I do know is that Chinese people are genuinely fascinated by and interested in all things Australian, be it our sportspeople (they loved Ian Thorpe and the size of his feet), art and landscapes (they all know Sydney and the opera house), or animals (I've seen lots of Chinese taxi drivers mime a kangaroo hopping – yes, while driving).

Likewise, we Australians are motivated to know and learn more about China.

I heard just recently about a private art gallery in Sydney that was preparing for an exhibition in a Beijing gallery – so now we are buying each other's art and hanging it in our homes. This kind of cultural exchange will happen more and more in the future, I hope.

Mixed marriages

I haven't found many books on mixed marriages. I guess this is because while all marriages have their difficulties, Chinese people are often intensely private people who don't like to write about these things in books. They don't like to air their grievances publicly.

I have occasionally searched for memoirs of people in Chinese-Western marriages or for other books on the subject, but I've never found books that have been recent or meaningful or gone into the issues at the heart of a mixed marriage.

Personally, I endured some things during the early years of my marriage because I thought they resulted from a cultural clash. After a few years of denying the problem, and then after some counselling, I realised that I needed to stand up for my beliefs regarding how I want to be treated. I realised I needn't accept things that go against my beliefs just because my husband has a different cultural background.

I have also learnt that my habit of being very direct and airing my emotions whenever I like may not always be in the best interests of my relationships. I've discovered that finding the right time to discuss issues makes a massive difference. Learning this has improved our marriage in recent years.

I've realised that the differences between our cultures are great. We need to make space in our relationship for these differences to exist. My wish for our children is that they take pride in both their Chinese background and their Australian way of life.

DISPLAYS OF PHYSICAL AFFECTION

Chinese people are generally restrained when it comes to physical displays of affection.

They tend to be fairly reserved when it comes to reaching out and touching and hugging and kissing the people they love. I have grown up with a fair amount of cuddles and kisses in our family, and I see this as a normal way to show my love and affection as I feel it expresses the joy that comes from my relationships with people in my family.

Chinese people, meanwhile, demonstrate their affection for each other by showing concern about what their loved ones are wearing (to check they will not be too hot or too cold), or something more practical, such as checking whether they've eaten.

My Chinese friends eventually got used to me wanting to give them a kiss on the cheek to greet them, as we do in Australia. When I lived in Beijing, I had lots of European friends and when we met we would kiss both cheeks in greeting. Some of our Chinese friends really like this custom, and don't shy away from shows of physical affection once they see it as normal. In China now, young lovers are fairly free with showing their physical love for each other in public.

Strangely enough, it is not unusual to see male friends displaying physical affection to each other in China. I often saw young male labourers happily walking down the street hand-in-hand.

Recently, during the London Olympics, I watched with interest the interactions between an Australian diver who won a silver medal and her coach (who was from a Chinese background), and compared them to the interactions between other Western divers and their Western coaches. On completing great dives, the divers were met poolside by their coaches. The

Western coaches freely embraced and hugged their divers, with lots of physical affection showing their joy. The Australian girl, meanwhile, reached out to hug her Chinese coach and was met with a reserved response in the early rounds. After the final round, he was more jubilant and hugged her more freely – but still nothing like the Western coaches.

CLEAN FEET

Clean feet are very important to Chinese people. In Australia, many of us go around in bare feet at home, out in the backyard and at the beach. We wear shoes if we are going out somewhere and if the ground is going to be hot (because it has been baked by the sun), or if there are prickles. In my backyard, I wear shoes so I don't stand in chicken poo. At the community kindergarten my children attend, children take their shoes off each day to play. The teachers actually require this, because the sensory stimulation that children receive from going barefoot indoors and outdoors is good for their brain development. I fear that Chinese children miss out on much of this, because they don't go barefoot outdoors ever.

We wear shoes for lots of reasons – not purely for the sake of keeping our feet clean, like the Chinese do. My husband is often horrified when he spies me lying on the bed reading with my feet in less than pristine condition. As a habit, my husband washes his feet every time he goes for a lie down. He can go without a shower easily, but will always, always wash his feet. The desire for lovely soft, clean feet is the reason why you will see Chinese women wearing thin stocking socks under their sandals in summer (even with a business suit). The stocking socks look terrible, but keep their feet "nice".

Aunties and Uncles

If you are a child walking on the street in China and you meet and speak to an adult, you will be prompted by your parent or grandparent to say, "Hello Aunty" or "Hello Uncle", even if the adult is a stranger. This respect for older people, where you always address a person older than you with a title, has its roots in Confucianism, which states that you must respect all people older than you, including teachers and your parents.

As a 21-year-old student in Beijing, I would call middle-aged women "Aunty" and older women "Old Person" (laorenjia 老人家), which is a respectful term. Now that I am approaching middle age, I am addressed as "Aunty".

Recently, while having lunch at Sunnybank, Brisbane's suburban Chinatown where all the local Chinese people go to eat, I encouraged my children (who are all seven and under) to call the waitress "Aunty". The waitress, who was probably in her late teens, giggled and said that they should call her "big sister". She didn't feel old enough to be their Aunty, and this made *me* feel old. She was putting herself in their generation and me in the one above. On the other hand, if you happened to address someone younger than you as "Aunty", it would be a terrible *faux pas*. You don't want to make someone feel older than they are!

Animal Zodiac

The importance of calling someone you meet by their respectful title means that you need to be pretty good at estimating people's ages. In Beijing, as foreign students, we travelled by taxi mostly (although I did resort to public transport when needed), and chatting with the taxi drivers gave us great opportunities to practise our Chinese. Beijingers love to chat. They would always want to guess my age or ask what animal year of the Chinese zodiac I was born in. I was initially curious about why they were interested in that… but I discovered that it is their way of confirming your age. If they know your sign, they can figure out how old you are, because the Chinese zodiac cycles through the animals in 12-year phases. Taxi drivers would want me to guess their age and I would try to be generous by taking some years off, but sometimes I would still be wrong. The long hours of working, day in, day out, without a break takes its toll, and so they often looked a lot older to me than they were.

Interestingly, in Qingdao, the taxi drivers don't talk as much. When I was dating my husband and struck up a conversation with a Chinese person who was a stranger to me, Shao Meng would discourage it. He was thinking: "Why would you want to talk to this person?" However, I think as a foreigner I was interested in talking to lots of people, as my way of getting more familiar with the culture and way of life. When we came to Australia, the roles were reversed, and I would wonder why my husband was not more discerning about whom he chatted with when he would strike up a conversation with some stranger.

So it is worth being aware that when a Chinese person is making conversation and asking you if you've heard of the Chinese animal years, they are just are trying to work out how old you are. They know it is rude to ask your age, so they'll talk about the Chinese zodiac. At least if someone asks you your star sign, they can't figure out how old you are!

Your salary is public knowledge

In China, everyone knows what everyone else is earning – although this is beginning to change. It is not uncommon to be asked straight out how much you earn as the first or second question when you meet someone new. This is very different in Australia. You might try to guess how much someone is earning by determining their job and their employer, but you would never ask someone how much they earn. It becomes really awkward when you make friends with a Chinese person in China (even your colleague) and they ask your salary. Even when I wasn't earning a high wage by Western standards, it was considerably higher than local salaries. If you don't admit your salary, it is considered rude but if you do give it, a look of shock will likely flash across their face.

Chinese are not very good at keeping these things private – just as they don't seem to take too well to a private ballot. In village elections, United Nations election workers have trouble enforcing secrecy at the ballot box.

Calcium in the Chinese diet

The main sources of calcium in most Western diets are dairy products (milk, yoghurt, cheese and ice cream). However, the Chinese traditionally haven't consumed much dairy at all. This has changed, however, and milk and yoghurt are now more common in people's diets. Traditionally, calcium in their diets came from eating whole, small bony fish, drinking soup made from pork or chicken bones (the calcium in the bones leeches out into the soup during cooking), eating prawn shells and tofu, and drinking soy milk.

Amusingly, Chinese people often told me that they knew the government gave out milk in Australia. The story goes like this:

When I was in China, someone would ask me my nationality, and I would say I was Australian. The Chinese person would then ask me if I was given free milk at school. I had no idea what they were talking about until I learnt about the Commonwealth government program in Australia in the 50s and 60s that provided milk to children at school. This was common knowledge in China in the 90s – Australia's solid welfare state is very well known. Many people in China thought that the program had continued to this day, so I would tell them that it is not provided now.

I would often hear that I was lucky because Australia was a rich country. Many commented that even if you don't work, you are still paid in Australia. Social welfare in Australia is in great contrast to China, which has a very weak welfare state for a communist country.

Chinese people pay for education and health care. There is no such thing as free schooling or Medicare, even if you are very poor. Chinese people seem to know all about our welfare payments and I do think some people want to immigrate to Australia, even if they don't speak English, because they think they can get money from the government without having to work (not just because Australia is such a beautiful place).

CUTE BABIES

Have you ever stopped to admire a tiny Chinese baby and thought they were particularly cute? My mother travelled to China in 1996 (the year before I first went) and came home raving about how cute the babies and toddlers were. Her experience is not unique, either. There is something especially cute about babies from China, I think. And the same is true in reverse: Chinese people will stop and stare and goo and ga over foreign babies. They want to hold them, make them smile, touch them and have their picture taken with them. They will also tell you every time that your baby is not wearing enough! I think they have a great tendency to overdress their babies!

Never Going Thirsty

In China, when you go to someone's office, workplace, or house, you will almost immediately be served a hot beverage. You don't have to know the people well. You won't necessarily be asked if you would like a drink, or what kind of beverage you would prefer. Most likely, you'll be served Chinese tea in a plastic cup. The Chinese tealeaves will be floating on the top of the drink, so you have to wait for them to sink to the bottom of the cup, or slurp past them if you are parched and can't wait for that to happen. This is very comforting, especially in winter. It means you don't have to carry your own water. It gives you something to do while you wait when you are doing business, and it is a basic courtesy.

Here in Australia, you would only be offered a hot drink in someone's house or in a workplace if you were staying a while, but in China the tea arrives immediately. In Australia, you are likely to be offered refrigerated water. Most Chinese people don't drink iced water because they believe in Chinese medicine, which counsels that our stomachs can't handle the cold. In fact, most of them don't drink water at room temperature, either. They drink only plain, hot water. Have you tried it? Once you are used to it, it is quite refreshing. Living in China, where you don't get to choose your hot drink, you take it as it comes. I found this made me much less fussy about how I like hot drinks when I came back from China. I can drink tea or coffee with or without milk, with or without sugar, and I really enjoy Chinese tea. I'm not fussy, which is considered good manners in China. In Australia, it is usual to be particular about how you drink your hot drinks. I do find that lots of Australians are adventurous and enjoy Chinese tea with their yum cha (which literally means "drink tea" in Cantonese), but I also know many people who don't stray from their standard tea with milk and two sugars. Most Chinese people don't ever drink coffee or black tea (which is called red tea or English tea in China).

Australia's ambassador to China spoke recently at a lecture in Brisbane. She mentioned that Queensland's tourism body, Tourism Queensland, had made some very practical recommendations to hotels hosting Chinese tourists. The first one was that they needed to provide Thermoses of boiled drinking water in all the rooms. Chinese people want to walk in and drink straight away. This is critical. That is what they expect. With the growing numbers of Chinese tourists coming to Australia, hotels need to start catering to their needs in order to build the tourist trade between our two countries.

People and Restaurants Everywhere

After a long bush walk in Australia, you probably come back to the place where you parked your car feeling wet and cold and tired and hungry (or hot and tired and hungry, depending on the season). You then take from your backpack a small picnic, maybe a sandwich and a piece of fruit, to be washed down with water or a Thermos of tea if you are lucky.

In China, after your adventures – whether you've climbed a mountain, seen a giant Buddha or hiked along a gorge – at lunchtime, wherever you are, you will always find a restaurant ready and waiting to cook you a lovely hot meal. The more remote the place, the more likely you are to have lovely home-style cooking. This is the best thing about living in China. Wherever you are, you can always get a nutritious hot meal (sometimes greasy and very salty and perhaps with too much MSG for some people), usually for a reasonable price and just when you really want it. Hooray for China's food culture!

The Beauty of Steam

I love walking along in China and seeing the steam rising up from the bamboo steam pots containing baozi (steamed dumplings), or from a rice pot or vat of noodles. I really think it is a thing of great beauty. Sitting in a cold kitchen (kitchens are not usually well heated in Northern China), in the middle of winter, watching the steam coming off a wok as lunch is cooking is a very comforting thing. Going onto the street and buying a big bowl of noodles and seeing the steam puffing up around you with a fabulous aroma is wonderful. Food is everywhere in China. The Chinese do have some great cold dishes, but there is no such thing as an entirely cold meal. My husband often has the sandwiches I cut for his lunch and he tolerates them, but what he really wants is a hot meal, every meal. And you know, most times that's what I want, too.

INFREQUENT SHOWERING

Ever wondered how Chinese people maintain their silky, wrinkle-free skin? As well as being born with good skin, the Chinese are very conscious of keeping it nice. Eating pork fat, according to the Chinese, is good for your skin. It makes it smooth and plump and healthy. My parents-in-law shower only a couple of times a week, and this is considered normal. Each evening they will have a wash, but they resist the urge to jump in the shower daily or even twice daily as lots of Westerners do. They say that over-washing will lead to skin complaints. I know I would not need so much moisturiser for my skin if I showered less often. Most of us know that if we have a long, hot shower in winter, it dries out our skin, but we do it anyway because it feels good. I definitely need daily showers.

Now, I'll admit there are some Chinese people who take it too far, and you sometimes run into people who clearly haven't showered for far too long – they have greasy hair, crumpled clothes that haven't been changed for weeks, and they smell. I've seen these Chinese people at university in China and in the offices I've worked at, but mostly you notice them when you are in confined spaces, like a lift.

But here's an interesting fact: Chinese people don't wear deodorant. And if they wash regularly, they don't smell. The Chinese do not have an offensive body odour. You don't see deodorant on the shelves in shops. All foreigners who are living in China take a stash of deodorant with them for their stay, or seek it out in foreign chemists.

There are still lots of poor people in China: over 50% are classed as rural peasants living on a very low income, as low as US$300 a year. They may shower only once a year, on Chinese New Year. The rest of the year they swim in the river, and that's it for washing.

In the cities, there are communal shower houses where you pay a fee to shower. Middle and higher income households all have their own showers now, but people may still go out for a shower to be pampered, and it is often a social occasion. They may have a facial, or have their feet scrubbed and massaged.

Chinese people are not all short

I once ran into the Chinese international women's volleyball team at an airport in China. I am a tall woman, but these strong, lean, toned, exceedingly tall women dwarfed me. They looked amazing as a team travelling together. All eyes were drawn to them. There is just something alluring and fascinating about a team of fit sportspeople (I saw a whole rugby league team on a plane in Australia once, too, and they looked mammoth).

Anyway, the point is that Chinese people are not all short. My husband is taller than I am. He's from Qingdao in the North of China. Qingdao is a lovely coastal city in Shandong Province. The tallest of the Chinese hail from Shandong. The Shandong people are the big Han Chinese (there are actually 56 minority groups in China, and Han is the largest group). My mother-in-law says that this is because wheat is the staple in the North. In the South, where rice is the staple food, people are less likely to be tall. In days gone by, most of the Chinese people leaving China for the West came from the Southern coastal provinces, hence the overseas Chinese population were typically not very tall. As a result, many Westerners think that all Chinese people are not very tall. And this is just not true!

Height is very important in China. One of the first things my father in-law said about me, in my favour, when he first met me was how tall I was. He was thinking this fared well for our potential offspring. To be tall in China is seen as an advantage.

100-DAY-OLD BIRTHDAY

All babies in China celebrate their 100th birthday – 100 days old, that is! In less fortunate times, when babies were more likely to die when they were little, having a baby survive his or her first 100 days was something to celebrate. The tradition is carried on today, and a fancy dinner is held. When my babies turned 100 days old, I baked each of them a little cake with "100" written on it.

At this 100-day mark, Chinese parents shave the baby's head. They do this because they believe it ensures the hair grows back thick and strong. They think these effects last a lifetime. We didn't shave our babies' heads – we let it stay baby-like and wispy.

One of the advantages to being married to a Chinese man is that we actually have double the celebrations (the Chinese term "double happiness" really does apply to us). We celebrate both Christmas and Chinese New Year, and hold a 100-days party as well as a Western-style naming ceremony for our babies after they are born. How lucky is that?

The Fourth Trimester

What's the first thing a mother does after giving birth to her baby? Maybe she'll breastfeed her new infant, or have a well-deserved cup of tea with a piece of toast, and then sleep. She will also, of course, have a lovely hot shower. Well, no such luck for a Chinese woman who is being nursed through the first month of her new babe's life!

According to the Chinese way, after giving birth new mothers are treated to an entire month of bed rest to sleep with and feed their baby. Sound ideal? Well, it is for the mother-baby bonding process and for establishing breastfeeding. They don't have to cook or wash or do anything around the house. Or, should I say, they are not *permitted* to do anything around the house. They are not allowed to do anything, including showering. Can you imagine that? For a whole month after childbirth, they are not allowed to shower. They are only allowed to have sponge baths.

The reason behind this ritual is that a woman's body is thought to be very vulnerable after birth. This I'm not disputing! A woman's body is recovering from being pregnant for nine months and from childbirth itself. However, to my mind, not permitting a woman to shower is my idea of torture.

Other rules during the confinement period include: no TV, no reading, and no sitting in a draft (i.e. no fresh air – windows stay shut). Apparently, sitting in a draft causes a woman's teeth to fall out when she gets older – or so the old wives' tale goes!

Now, fortunately for me, my mother-in-law doesn't believe in all of this. She boastfully declares that she had a shower straight after she birthed her two children, and did all the washing in the first month, too.

When my mother-in-law came to stay with us after the birth of my third child, she treated me to lots and lots of time alone with my newborn, to rest and sleep and feed and bond. My mother-in-law rushed around, washing and cooking and cleaning and playing with my older children in order to care for me. This was fabulous.

My mother and my younger sister helped immensely when my other children were born with cooking and washing and shopping, but it wasn't live-in and around-the-clock help, as it was with my mother-in-law.

Central Kingdom

The literal translation of the two words that make up China mean "Central Kingdom". This explains a lot, I think. To the Chinese, China is the country in the middle and all the other countries in the world are positioned around them. Some Chinese characters are pictograms, so they are actually pictures that tell you what the word means. The two characters for the word "China" are both pictograms. The first character, "middle" (中), is a vertical stroke with a rectangular box around the central section of the stroke, indicating the middle. The character for "kingdom" (国), which is now used to mean "country" as well, is a rectangle representing a border with a picture of a king inside.

With China's long recorded history on earth and advanced early civilisation, it is a proud nation. Given this, it is not surprising that many Chinese genuinely believe they are the centre of the world. This probably explains a bit about the way they conduct themselves politically in the world today.

WHITE IS BEAUTY

Every time my husband sees a Caucasian model with a deep tan, he shakes his head. He can't understand why they would want to get a tan. The idea that it makes a woman more attractive eludes him. For Westerners, a tan traditionally conjures up images of a long summer holiday spent soaking up sun. Now with our knowledge of skin cancer, many tans we see are fake. This is even more puzzling for my husband. You see, in China, it is the reverse. Chinese people are always thinking: How can I make my skin a few shades whiter? In Australia, there's a massive market for fake tan; in China, there is a massive market for skin whitener. Traditionally in China, you had a tan if you were a peasant farmer who was out in the field working all day. Only the aristocrats had time to shade their skin and keep out of the sun and consequently stay white. Sunscreen is popular in China now, not because of skin cancer, but because of their desire to stay white.

I sometimes wondered, in some of China's most polluted cities, if any UV rays would make it through the layers of polluted gases in the atmosphere, anyway.

Chinese New Year

Chinese New Year is also called Spring Festival. It is the official start of spring on the lunar calendar, so it falls on a different date every year because it is determined by the timing of the full moon. Traditionally, it is the start of a new year, when the weather is warming after a long, cold winter. It is a time of renewal, and the Chinese celebrate by gathering together with their family and eating and drinking. It is the one time of the year when Chinese people don't spare any expense. They celebrate by buying new clothes and shoes to wear on the first day of the new year, and by buying fireworks and letting them off (the louder, the better). In the city, on Chinese New Year there are fireworks for three days straight, all day and night. And they are loud. You can barely hear yourself speak indoors for the noise of the fireworks and firecrackers outside. People often find particularly cavernous places to let them off for maximum volume and impact: a concrete stairwell or courtyard, for example.

Older relatives give out lucky red packets with wads of cash inside to the younger people in the family. This is called "squash the age" money – in other words, money that ensures the children won't grow up too quickly.

Children eat lollies, and go to their Aunties' and Uncles' houses to wish them a happy new year and eat good food. In the North, everyone eats jiaozi (a simple handmade boiled dumpling, made with wheat flour and filled with pork mince).

Having sons

In 1997, I spent the summer holidays travelling by sleeper train around China. Staring out the window of the train as it passed through village after village, I read lots of the government propaganda – large red characters stencilled onto white village walls all around the country, portraying government messages to the masses. At first glance, it looked to me like graffiti. But once I'd seen the same message enough times, it dawned on me. This was government propaganda.

One I remember and saw often was: "Sons and daughters are the same." The intention of this message from the government was to encourage parents to treasure all their children, whether male or female.

My father, who has three girls, can't understand why there is a need to do this. He loves having three daughters. I think he feels really sad that people cannot love their daughters as they would sons. I try to explain it to him.

Traditionally in China, if you had a daughter it meant you had to feed and raise a child, which is an expensive process. When the daughter was older, she helped around the farm, but as soon as she reached a suitable age she was married and became part of her husband's family. She then returned once a year for one day, on the third day of the Chinese New Year. Not a great return on your investment!

However, if you had a son, you fed and raised a child – which is expensive – but when he was older, he helped around the farm and when he eventually married, you gained a new daughter-in-law. You then had a son and a daughter-in-law to work on the farm and raise children of their own. The son and his wife remained part of your family. They were with you for the Chinese New Year feast and the rest of the year. So a son was like two for the price of one.

This is a traditional outlook and the attitude is changing, but for the millions of poor Chinese villagers, while they love their offspring, having children is a way of surviving. They don't have the choices and ability to do what they want. They are living hand-to-mouth.

Daily visits to the fresh food market

In China, it is wonderful that, in any city, there is a market within walking distance of your house. At the markets, you can buy fresh meat, fish, vegetables, fruit, eggs and freshly-made noodles. The market is open all day and you can buy your ingredients to make your lunch and dinner. Your food is fresh. Cook some rice in the rice cooker, wash and chop your meat and veggies, fry a couple of dishes up in the wok (with a good spoonful of MSG and salt, and always garlic, ginger and spring onions or leek), and you've got yourself a cheap and healthy Chinese-style diet. Simple and tasty!

The cooking and daily visit to the market is usually performed by someone in the house: Mum, Dad, Grandma or Grandpa, or Aunty. In a wealthy household, it may be a hired helper who shops, but this daily task is always done by someone. Oh, I find this option so much nicer than a big weekly shop at the supermarket. With the high population density, there is enough business to sustain a market near everyone. The big population creates a great sense of social connection between the people, too. And you can buy just what you feel like at the time. I love it when I'm in Qingdao, staying with my parents-in-law: before someone goes off to the market, they ask what dishes we'd like today, and we can request our favourites. Yum!

ACTIVE LIVES

Just as people walk to their local market to buy their fresh produce, they usually walk to and from the bus stop on their daily commute to work. The number of well-off people who have cars and drive around town to work and to supermarkets is growing, but they are still in the minority. Life is not as sedentary as it is in Australian cities.

In Beijing, the topography is flat, so it is a great city for riding a bicycle. You can ride anywhere; there are no hills at all. People ride their bikes everywhere, no matter what the weather. When it rains, they have awesome hooded raincoats which cover their arms and their work bag in the front basket.

In summer in Hangzhou, I've seen women wearing beautiful silk covers on their arms to keep the sun off when they ride their bikes. It is so practical. They seem not to care what it looks like.

In winter in the North, they rug up with feather puffer jackets, scarves, hats, gloves and long johns. In the spring dust storms, they wrap chiffon scarves over their faces to keep the dust out of their eyes, noses and mouths. And so they can ride whatever the weather.

Most residential housing in China is usually about six storeys high. This is the maximum number of floors you can have without installing a lift, according Chinese building regulations. So people often have to climb many steps up to their home, carrying the shopping. This active lifestyle is good for people socially too, I think, as you see people walking on the streets saying hi to their neighbours and going about their business.

It is probably one of the major reasons why there is such a low rate of obesity among adults in China. In 2008, the World Health Organisation measured the Chinese adult obesity rate at under 10%, whereas in the US this rate is more than 30%. These rates are, however, increasing. As more Chinese people drive around in cars eating Western junk food, obesity rates are growing quickly. Which leads me to my next point!

LITTLE EMPERORS

The obesity rate among children in China is growing at an alarming rate. This is potentially due to their single-child policy, and lots of relatives feeding their few grandchildren an abundance of treats.

The one-child policy has resulted in many second-generation single children who have six family members doting over them. The one-child policy was introduced in 1980 in an attempt to slow down population growth, and it has been effectively enforced. (The government introduced this policy because Mao Zedong had, earlier in the century, attempted to build the biggest army in the world for national security, by encouraging population growth to such an extent that the resultant rate of growth was unsustainable.)

The government enforces the one-child policy by linking people's employment to their fertility control. People with their own businesses may not have to worry about limiting the number of children they have, but they will face a hefty fine and will have to pay high school fees for their extra children. For instance, I've recently made a new Chinese friend who was born in 1980, and she is the oldest in her family. She was born just after the one-child policy was introduced. She is one of five children – she has three younger sisters and one younger brother. Her brother is the fifth child. Her paternal Grandma desperately wanted a grandson, so her parents kept having babies until they had a boy. They had to pay fines, but they had a factory that was doing well, so they could afford it.

The one-child policy is well enforced and is very, very sad for many people. One of my husband's good friends and his wife had a son, but wanted to have another baby. He had a good job with a company that had links to a state-owned enterprise. They were well off, so could easily afford to raise two children. They became pregnant, but the wife was visited by her husband's boss, who said that her husband would lose his great job and his pleasant lifestyle if they had the second baby. They felt they had no choice but to abort the much-wanted baby. This is a very sad story, but also a very common occurrence.

So, back to the little emperors in the cities. Their parents usually keep working once they've had the baby, meaning two incomes and one child. The two sets of grandparents will usually both assist with child-raising. This means there are six doting adults for each little child. Needless to say, a lot of Chinese children are spoiled rotten – hence they get the name "little emperors". They don't learn how to help with the chores and they are treated to their favourite foods, as all the grown-ups compete for time with and attention from their one offspring. They have no siblings or cousins to share toys with; just an abundance of food and material possessions to fill their time.

Good health

As a parent, I know to be grateful for every day that I am healthy and my children are healthy. It is the days when one of us is sick when I really wonder if I may have gotten myself in too deep by having three children in quick succession. Then I remind myself that we are healthy most of the time, and that it is normal to be sick occasionally. I take care of what needs doing, rest and distract myself with a good book, and try not to think too much.

From what I've observed, the Chinese really understand the importance of a healthy mind and body. When they meet a friend or a family member, they'll ask, "How's your body?" (meaning, "Are you healthy?"). They will then ask after the family's health, and the last thing they might say when you won't be seeing each other for a while is: "Pay attention to your body" (meaning, "Take care of your health"). At the dinner table, "good health" is a popular toast.

DISCRETIONARY SPENDING

It always struck me as different, the way Chinese people exercised their discretion and chose to spend their money. Their priorities always seemed slightly different to mine. For example, I might be picked up by a Chinese friend's family in a lovely new car, only to step into their house to find the bathroom has a broken tap and a toilet that doesn't work, so you have to try to flush with a container of water which you dip into a pre-prepared bucket of water. A young work colleague carried the latest expensive mobile phone, but when I went to her apartment, the concrete floor was bare and had absolutely no floor covering. This pattern is consistent with the idea that when you go onto the street, you have to look good, but when you go home it doesn't matter. Coming from my background – and maybe it is my English heritage – you want everything to be working in your house first before you splash out on the latest a mobile phone. We put a lot of emphasis on having a comfortable home, and we like to invite our friends over. I've observed that the Chinese are a lot less likely to invite people over, so don't be offended if you aren't invited to a Chinese friend's house. They are more likely to entertain at a restaurant.

They may also spend a lot of money on a very expensive gift to show that they are doing well financially, and then behind closed doors eat only vegetables and rice for a week because they can't afford meat.

These examples illustrate the concept of preserving "face". How things look in public, how well educated you are and how much money you have are very important to Chinese people, as these are signs that they are achieving well.

Barbers on the street

When I first went to China in 1997, I thought it was really strange to see barbers working on the street corners. The barbers bring out their tools, a stool and a cape and wait on the street for their customers. The hair just falls onto the ground. They save on rent, but I can't think of many advantages to having my hair cut in the street. Here in Australia, you'd get sunburnt. I think I would feel self-conscious having my hair cut in full view of everyone (and being China, there are lots and lots of people to see – whole bus loads of people driving by, for instance). Remember too that since I am a foreigner in China, this causes people to stare at me anyway.

Sitting next to the road to have your hair cut is an example of the Chinese people's lack of a need for privacy. Dentists, although they don't work on a street corner, always have wide glass windows to allow people to stare in at the patient having work done. In hospitals, meanwhile, it is not unusual for people to crowd around you while you are consulting with the doctor.

Special names for relatives

In China, your Dad's mum is called "Nai Nai" (pronounced Nigh Nigh). "Nai" is actually the Chinese character for milk. I think this is a lovely connection. Your Grandma is as important to you as milk. I wonder about the root word from which the English term "Nanna" derives, because the two names – Nanna and Nai Nai – are very similar. There is usually a close bond that develops between the paternal grandmother and the child, because her son and her daughter-in-law traditionally live as a part of her household. If they were peasants, the child's mother would be free to work in the fields while Nai Nai took responsibility for the childcare activities.

So now we know how to refer to a child's paternal grandmother in Chinese. In fact, there is a special term for every relative in your family. You can be very precise: for example, you can specify the Aunty who is your father's younger sister ("Gu Gu"), and if there are two younger sisters, you can differentiate between your father's big younger sister ("Da Gu") and your father's little younger sister ("Xiao Gu"). Their husbands are referred to as "Da Gu Fu" ("Fu" meaning "husband") and "Xiao Gu Fu". A generic term like "Aunty" is used only for strangers.

As I mentioned, one of the main tenets of Confucianism is to continually demonstrate respect and care for people older than you, as well as for your teachers. This has been carried right into modern Chinese culture, where special terms for referring to relatives are still used.

Younger siblings will never call their older brothers and sisters by name, but by the term "Big Brother" or "Big Sister". If there is more than one older brother or sister, then they use the name followed by "Big Brother" or "Big Sister". My sister-in-law calls my husband "Ge" (for "Big Brother"), and I have a special name, too ("Saozi") – but she seldom uses it, probably because it feels weird using it to address a foreigner. However, she doesn't say my name either. She just leaves it out. You can't use simple personal pronouns like "you" or "your" or "his" or "her" when you are referring to older people in your presence – you use their title. For example, you don't say, "How are you, Mum?", you say, "How is Mum?"

Cousins and close family friends also call each other "brother" and "sister". You can call your children as the oldest, then number two, then number three etc. Admittedly, they use the word "Lao" in front of these numbers, which infers caring and closeness, so it doesn't sound as cold or inhumane as it does in English. This custom eliminates a lot of confusion, because everyone has a special name. A stranger can discuss your children with you without knowing their names.

Often in China, titles are used instead of given names. This can take some time to get used to, and I often feel I need to be very aware of who is who and what I should call them.

Climbing mountains

One Labour Day holiday weekend, I climbed Mount Tai in North China. I climbed thousands and thousands of steps along with thousands and thousands of Chinese people also making the most of the long weekend. It was crowded – so crowded that I couldn't put my foot on the next step until the person in front of me moved their foot. We were students exploring China and out for adventure, so that explains our desire to climb a very tall mountain. But what were all these Chinese people doing climbing the mountain in business suits, and some even in high heels? They were pursuing longevity. It is said that climbing Mount Tai will ensure that you live to a ripe old age.

"Cheers" means "scull"

In China, you say "gan bei" when you toast and raise your glass to someone. It means "dry cup". So to get a dry cup, you need to empty your cup, or "bottoms-up" or scull your drink down. In China, you are a good host if you can be sure that your guests have had a great feast and lots to drink. How can you tell if someone has had enough to drink? They'll be drunk, of course.

As the name suggests, rice wine is made from rice, and it takes a lot of rice to make rice wine. Traditionally, your guest knows you really respect them if you serve a big quantity of wine, because the rice that was used to make the wine would have fed the family for a long time. This need to "give face" and please your guests is very strong in China.

A Chinese dinner will normally involve lots of toasts in rapid succession during the course of the evening. The guests know when to start eating by following the host's lead, and people drink only when there is a toast. It is quite rigid – nothing like our dinners, when you drink as often and whenever you please. The dinner will go on for a couple of hours at the most, and then everyone goes home for an early night. None of this standing around in a bar with a beer in your hand for a few hours! This custom is changing among some young people, but the formal business dinner is still the most common way to entertain clients in China.

A KID'S EDUCATION

My oldest son is in his third year at primary school, so I have a few friends with children at school now. When I enquire about how their kid is doing at school, a parent might reply something like, "He loves it", "He likes soccer", "He's got a great teacher" or "The school seems to be really good". I know he is only in the lower grades, so it is a little early to be overly-concerned with academic achievement, but it is my experience that people are generally concerned with the whole picture: Are the kids happy? Is the teacher good? Is the school friendly?

This is not so in China. In China, when you ask about your friends' children, the pertinent question seems to be: How are they achieving at school? How are their studies going? There is a really strong emphasis on academic achievement. Parents with a low level of education will expect their children to study hard as a way of escaping a life of labour, where you work to live. My husband in particular has noticed that parents in Australia seem concerned with many different aspects of a child's development, with a lesser focus on academic achievement.

Pressure to settle down

In days gone by in China, if a woman was approaching her late 20s and she was not married or soon to be, her parents would go into a haze of melancholy, believing that their daughter would never marry. When I was in China 10 years ago, I had two lovely 30+ friends who were both very high achievers academically and professionally, but had not yet succeeded in finding husbands – and they were under a lot of pressure to do so.

Parents feel such distress in these circumstances because they worry that an eligible bachelor would not choose a 30-year-old bride when they could choose a much younger one. Men don't have the same age constraints placed on them when it comes to marriage.

The idea that a woman will get left on the shelf if she is not married before 30 still exists. I do think, however, that things are definitely relaxing on this front as time goes on. I know of two well-educated professional women from the city – my sister-in-law and my husband's cousin – who have just recently married in their early 30s.

What is the meaning of "good"?

The character for "good" in Chinese is a pictogram consisting of the picture for "woman" and the picture for "child". So a woman with a child represents what is good in the world.

HE OR SHE

If you have a Chinese friend and they often say "he" instead of "she" or vice versa, it is because "he", "she" and "it" are all pronounced the same way in Chinese. "Ta" means "he", "she" and "it" in Chinese. It is easy for an English speaker, because when you speak in Chinese your brain doesn't have to distinguish between these three pronouns. But in my experience, it doesn't matter how well or for how long a Chinese person speaks English, this is one small mistake they continually make. My husband does it, and my kids find it rather amusing. I find it endearing.

RAW NOODLES

On my wedding day in China, I had to act out a number of wedding rituals. One was to sit on the bed and eat noodles with chopsticks out of the same bowl as my husband. As we were slurping the noodles and feeding each other, slurping from opposite ends of the same noodle, the relatives were crowded around, taking photos and laughing and asking us very loudly: "Raw or not?" I had to shout back "raw". Actually, the noodles were not raw, but I had to say they were. This is because the written character for "raw" is the same as the written character for "have a baby". So by saying the noodles were raw, I was shouting out for all my husband's relatives that I would have babies. They all cheered. Such is the ritual for ensuring the new wife knows she should produce babies for the family.

Peanuts

The Chinese can be very superstitious: dates are significant, and following rituals at certain times is important to ensure you lead a prosperous and happy life.

We have a bunch of multi-coloured macramé peanuts hanging from our kitchen window. They are to ensure that we have a mixture of boys and girls in our offspring. The word for peanuts in Mandarin is pronounced "hua sheng". "Sheng" also means "to have a baby" and "hua" can mean "multi-coloured" – so the derived meaning explains that peanuts represent a birth order of boy, girl, boy, girl. It worked for our first two children: we had a boy and then a girl, and then we had another girl – we were of course delighted with the safe arrival of our healthy girls and we love all of our children dearly. (My husband did think that we'd have all boys – I don't know why.)

In Western culture, I think people are usually happy if they have a "pigeon pair" – meaning a girl and a boy – and they often stop there. People may feel a tad gibed if they miss out on a girl or a boy altogether. My Dad didn't feel that way at all – he had three girls. Generally, I think we are pretty flexible and happy with what we have. These days, for Chinese people who don't live a traditional life in the countryside, having a son doesn't really matter as much as it does in the villages. I had a colleague who was happy to have a daughter (knowing he was legally able to have only one child) because he thought girls were more obedient than boys.

Chilli

Chinese people like chillies, and not just because they enjoy hot food.

As well as a string of macramé peanuts in our kitchen, we have a bunch of silky red chillies hanging up in our spare room. My mother-in-law once explained the significance of the humble red chilli: red symbolises prosperity, wealth and good times in China. If your life is prosperous, it is thought to be plump and shiny and red and glossy – like a chilli. So Chinese people hang up bunches of fake chillies to bring good fortune to their lives.

Daughter's choice of husband

As I've mentioned earlier, when a Chinese girl is married, she becomes part of her new family and leaves her old family behind. On her wedding day, after she's been fed a big meal (in the North of China, this is a big meal of jiaozi, which are dumplings), she leaves her home for the last time, and she is not to look back at her parents as her new husband takes her off to her new life as a member of his family. Traditionally, she will return only once a year, on the third day of Chinese New Year.

It is for this reason that Chinese parents are very concerned about their daughter's choice of husband – not just because it determines who her husband will be, but because it will also determine what her whole life will be like. If her husband is a kind person but his family doesn't have much money, then her life will be difficult. If her husband is kind but his family is not, she might be treated badly by her new extended family for the rest of her life.

My husband's family were very welcoming of me and they treat me very well, so I'm one of the lucky ones. They put up with my faults and will do whatever they can to make my life easier and more comfortable. I can tell them my problems, and they are always asking if I need anything.

When Shao Meng and I were dating, his mother gave him money so he could take me out. She assured me that Shao Meng was a kind man, and gave examples to prove it to me.

A mother-in-law who doesn't listen to you or treats you badly in China can really make for a difficult life, so a girl's parents are very anxious to make sure their daughter's husband is from a good family. Arranged marriages are not very common in China today, but it is still normal for meetings with parents to be a sort of test. The parents have to like the new potential bride or groom for their son or daughter. The couple's parents often meet to determine if it is a good match and to make plans for the start of the marriage. Typically, the decision to get married is much more a family affair in China than it is in the West.

Wedding Day

On my wedding day in Qingdao, China, I wore four qipaos (traditional Chinese silk dresses which are fitted, long and straight, with long openings up the side of the leg). My mother-in-law had taken me off to a tailor who'd measured me up, helped me choose the silk and fitted me. The style I wore had intricate buttons. The wedding day is an occasion for the groom's parents to show off to their relatives and friends what a great bride their son has captured, and to display their wealth (to whatever degree) by dressing their new daughter-in-law up and parading her around. I enjoyed getting the hairdo suited for qipaos and having my Chinese bridal make-up painted on. I even wore embroidered silk slippers.

The first qipao I wore was bright red, with golden thread and capped sleeves. I then changed into a pale orange qipao which had a phoenix woven into the silk. The next one was bright aqua, with a gold and pink pattern. The last qipao, which I wore for the evening dinner, was light pink.

I adored wearing the gorgeous silk creations tailored especially for me. The wedding planner hired people with both video and photo cameras to follow us around all day, so we have a detailed record of our wedding day.

Ducks Swimming on the Pond

After our wedding in China, we came to Australia for our Australian wedding, which was also our legal wedding. Shao Meng's best friend, Wang Xiongwen, came to perform the role of best man. We flew into Brisbane and hired a car to drive up to Bargara for the wedding. On the way back, we stopped for a picnic at Gympie at a popular lakeside spot just off the highway. Ducks and many other varieties of birds live around the lake.

Shao Meng and Wang Xiongwen's eyes lit up. They both seemed to say "lunch" at precisely the same time. They seriously began to try their luck at catching a bird. They couldn't believe that these were wild ducks, happily roaming around, and no one was going to catch them to eat them. No wonder there is a shortage of wild birds in China.

Chinese people eat more parts of animals than Westerners usually do. While using the whole beast is becoming popular in some culinary corners of Australia (and was more popular historically in Australia), the Chinese have been doing it for centuries, often due to economic reasons. My husband loves shocking people by talking about eating pigs' stomachs (which are actually very tasty), or lambs' intestines (there is no disguising the smell or the taste of these!). Then there is the Chinese tradition of serving the duck's head along with the rest of the bird – I always tell the guy selling me the duck that I don't want the head.

EAT SLOWLY

When you get to the end of a dinner in China and you start to feel very full, your hosts will gently encourage you to "eat up". They are actually telling you to eat slowly: to keep eating, but to do so at a slower pace. It is part of the strategy to ensure they've been a great host, by making sure you are full.

Just as a Chinese friend will tell you to eat slowly, when you are leaving a friend's house or an office, the friend will say: "go slowly". They mean that you should go steadily and take care. By repeating these little phrases, Chinese people are encouraging each other to eat slowly, go slowly or not to rush. These gentle reminders are very kind, I think. I really enjoy saying, "go slowly" to Chinese friends or family, and I try to remember to do so myself.

My father-in-law exemplifies the benefits of slowing down. He has had a very successful career as part of the management team of a large textile machinery factory. He is a kind man who doesn't rush around. His actions are deliberate and thought through carefully. He eats slowly, making sure everyone else is getting their share of the food, and he'll be the last one at the table slurping his soup at the end of his meal.

Traditional Chinese food is slow food. There is nothing fast about making a feast of dumplings. You start with the flour and water to make the dough for the dumpling wrappers. Then you prepare the pork mince filling. Once those elements are ready, you hand-make each individual dumpling. Then you boil them and add cold water to the pot three times, waiting for it to boil after each addition of water.

The slow food movement may be popular now in the West, but I'd argue that the Chinese have always been slow food enthusiasts (although the growing popularity of Western fast food outlets in China is a worry, as are the big tummies on lots of the spoilt only-children). Relaxing and enjoying your food, without rushing, can have profound benefits.

Slow down and enjoy the moment.

Living life by passing the days

From my view, it seems the Chinese are pretty good at taking each moment as it comes, without needing to be entertained or stimulated all of the time. When it is time to make dinner, there is a single-minded focus on preparing the meal. My mother-in-law sits or stands in her modest kitchen, separating the coriander stems one at a time in silence. She doesn't listen to the radio while she works, or talk on the phone. Then when it is time, one eats. Then after lunch, you can have a nap. You don't feel like you are missing out on anything – you rest to make your body feel good for the remainder of the day. In this way, a day passes, and in the same way the next day passes, and this is what makes up your life. It is a steady way to live a calm and peaceful life.

When my husband talks to his friends on the phone and they ask him about his exciting life in Australia, he laughs it off and says it is just passing the days – going to work, exercising and spending time with the children. That is what life is about.

Women hold up half the sky

Chinese men are pretty helpful around the house. In China, you will often see fathers or grandfathers taking children to school on the backs of their bikes. On special occasions, the man of the house will usually step into the kitchen to cook up a storm.

My father-in-law helps my mother-in-law with the spring clean each year before Chinese New Year. He scrubs grease from around the cooker in the kitchen and cleans the windows.

I guess this is partly because of the communist influences in the country. The famous Mao slogan, "women hold up half the sky", dictated that women would have to go to work just like the men. They did get paid maternity leave, but had to return to full-time work just a few months after their baby was born. My mother-in-law was working in a large government-owned machinery factory on the banks of the Yangtze River (which is known as "Chang Jiang" in Chinese), and it was run like a big commune. Everyone had an apartment, and most services were provided by the factory. There was a factory school and a factory nursery where the babies were cared for. Luckily, my mother-in-law was able to go and breastfeed her son and daughter at lunchtime. It was a hard life. My mother-in-law explains that it was extremely tiring to have to work full-time, then come home and do all the mothering and cooking and washing. My father-in-law had to attend lots of communist party meetings, and so she would have to do all the work at home as well. Because of the overwhelming nature of these demands, when she had a second child, a daughter, she chose to send her off to the grandparents' house, a long way away in Qingdao. She was raised by them until she could go to pre-school, as the conditions in the factory nursery were very poor. This was a very difficult thing to do. When I've talked to her about this, she told me how she missed her daughter dearly, but she thought it was the best thing for the child. It has affected their relationship. There is a distance that I see between them – they are not as close as they would have been if Shao Kun had not been sent away.

Back to the present: my husband does most of the washing up in our house. But that isn't to say that there aren't a few more chores I'd be happy if he took on!

Don't flip the fish!

Fish is nearly always on the menu in China. In Qingdao, the fish is the last dish to come to the table, and is usually served whole. It may have been steamed or stewed or fried or roasted, and will always come with some delectable sauce; my favourite kind is whole steamed fish. Shao Meng likes to buy a whole snapper on weekends now, which he steams and finishes off with some hot flavoured oil that he pours over at the end.

As is the usual custom with dining in China, the food is put in the middle and then everyone digs in with their chopsticks. When you eat a whole fish and you finish the top side, there is then the back bone, and the meat underneath the fish left to enjoy. It seems natural that you would just flip the fish over and go for the other side – but this is not considered to be a lucky act at all. It is actually better manners just to do your best to pick the fish out with your chopsticks and then wait for someone to remove the backbone so that everyone can eat the fish on the underside. Superstition has it that if you flip the fish, the next time you are in a boat it will capsize, or your car may overturn. Not a good outcome! Notably, fishermen and taxi drivers are very careful not to flip their fish.

THE RED THREAD

The Chinese believe in fate and the idea that lovers are tied together with an invisible red thread. This thread signifies that no matter what happens, they have always been destined to be together.

"Deeds not Words"

This is the school motto of the local state school that my children attend here in Australia.

My father-in-law likes to judge people based on how they live up to this motto. He categorises people based on whether they know how to talk the talk, and whether they know how to do the work required. So by his reckoning, there are people who know how to talk: they are charming and considerate and impress people with what they have to say. Then there are the people who know how to get the job done. The ultimate goal, then, is to know how to communicate well *and* get the job done. There are people who are great workers, but don't get far because they can't follow through with the required etiquette and reasoning required to communicate well. And we've all met the ones who talk themselves up and then are not actually able to do what they've promised.

I think that remembering you need both these qualities to be successful stands you in good stead. Maybe the school motto should be "Deeds *and* Words"?

Red packet

At weddings, the guests bring money for the bridal couple in a red packet. At Chinese New Year, when a child wishes their Aunties and Uncles and Grandparents a Happy New Year, they are rewarded with money in a red packet. When a woman agrees to marry, she is given money in red packets from her new parents. I received lots of lucky amounts when I married my husband: US$666.66 and then for good measure, I was given 666.66 yuan in another red packet. Six is a number that is believed to help things go smoothly. The reason for this is that "six" sounds the same as "smoothly" in Chinese.

Nine is also lucky number, because it means "forever". Eight is a lucky number because the figure 8 turned on its side is the symbol for infinity, and this indicates that you will be rich. On the unlucky side, four is also the word for "dying", so Chinese people don't usually like it. A number with two in it is auspicious for weddings, because it represents a pairing. Wedding dates are set by fortune-tellers, who know which days are lucky. This is a big deal: you have to make sure the date is lucky in the lunar calendar and also lucky in the regular calendar. Fortune-tellers are also consulted for help in choosing a name for new babies. The date you are born on helps to determine which character will be lucky for your name, and the meaning of the name for Chinese people is more important than how it sounds.

Pear superstition

The Chinese word for "pear" is pronounced the same as the word for "separate". So Chinese people won't sit down with their friends or family and cut a pear into pieces and share it, because this is bad luck. It means that you and the person you are sharing the pear with will separate. Likewise, if two lovers decide to go their separate ways, they may well sit down and share a pear to symbolise the separation.

BIG HOME

The word for "everyone" in Chinese is "big home" – the first character means "big" and the second character means "home". To include everyone, then, is to put them all into a big home. This is a very inclusive and kind meaning, I think. It demonstrates the generosity and kindness that I often experienced in China, where I was made to feel like we are all in this together.

Handing over money for nothing

On the other hand, Chinese people have an underlying lack of trust for people they do not know well. In China, gambling is illegal. Raffles are unheard of – even charity raffles. I remember when Shao Meng and I first came to Australia together and we went to a pub. The local rotary club was raising money by raffling a meat tray. Shao Meng was very puzzled. He thought: Why are all these people handing over their money? He did not feel that the diners should put their trust in the ticket sellers to do the right thing, and he made some comment about how this was stealing. He thought they'd get the money and leave without drawing a winner or providing the promised meat tray. In China, insurance companies are known to be very good at collecting the premiums, but are notorious for not paying claims. Raffles and insurance are typically not reasons to hand over money in China.

Thanks for having a son

When I gave birth to my son Elliot, my mother-in-law thanked me. She actually said the words: "Thank you for having a son for us." This is not something anyone else said to me when I had a son. I was having a baby for my family, but primarily for my husband and myself. To think that I had done some great duty in providing a son for my husband's family gave me a funny feeling, because it was an amazing privilege for me to give birth to a healthy child. It was challenging to take on the role of primary provider for a tiny human, but it was rewarding and fulfilling in equal amounts, and so I didn't need to be thanked for it. But imagine receiving an amazing gift of a healthy baby, and being thanked for it, too! That's a good gig! I am a lucky daughter-in-law in a Chinese family who produced a son.

A TALL NOSE

In the *Hansel and Gretel* storybook CD that my daughter enjoys, there is a line about the ugly witch, and to describe just how ugly the witch is, the book says: "She has a nose as long as her broomstick." In Western culture, long noses are not nice. In fact, given that your nose grows your whole life, having a long nose is not something to be pleased about.

But this is not how a long nose is seen in the eyes of the Chinese. I have a long nose and I am definitely not proud of it, but I accept it as the one I've been given. One of my high school friends asked me if I'd get a nose job, and the answer was and always will be: *no,* I will definitely not get a nose job. As it turns out, my long nose is appreciated in China. The Chinese don't say "long nose", by the way – they say "tall nose", which actually sounds better to me.

Anyway, I would often hear people say, "Wow, look how tall her nose is." The people who said this within earshot seemed to assume that I didn't understand Chinese, since even though having a tall nose is not an insult in China, I don't think they would have made such outright comments about someone's appearance if they knew they could be heard and understood. My tall nose is talked about in China. Chinese people often can be heard complaining about having a flat nose. So there you are! I figure at least our children won't have noses that are too long by Western standards, or too flat by Chinese standards – they will have "just-right" noses. When my third child, a daughter, was born, my mother-in-law met her on the day of her birth. She went on and on about how tall her nose was, even though she had just been born. Did you know that newborn babies have flat noses that perk up after a few days? Anyway, my daughter does have a lovely nose.

Students' pastimes

One of my expatriate friends in China, a teacher, always expressed dismay at China's university students' lack of wholesome pastimes. On a Monday morning, to kick-start some conversation practice, she would question her students about what activities they'd been involved in over the weekend. The most common response was, "watch TV". Watching TV is the major pastime in many Chinese people's lives. Admittedly, there are over 50 free satellite television channels available in the country. I wonder if this is due in part to it being a free activity, as Chinese people don't like to spend too much money. But it would have been heartening if one of them had said that they went bush walking or rollerblading or volunteering or something else, rather than just TV watching. My husband likes to drink Chinese tea and watch TV – we do get him out and he does enjoy outings, but he longs to be at home watching TV. I go stir crazy if I spend more than two hours locked inside with the TV on, so I tend to leave him to it.

A SPARE PATCH

Lots of people enjoy gardening in Australia, and this includes planting a vegetable patch in the backyard and maybe a fruit tree or two if there is a suitable spot, as well as a few pots of herbs on the verandah. When Chinese people come to Australia (in particular older people who were raised in households where it was the norm to grow their own food), they often buy themselves a small suburban block of land and really go to town with the gardening. Or should I say farming? Almost every spare inch is used for growing something: chillies, Chinese greens, gourds, beans… The front flower garden is converted into three utilitarian rows of greens. Water used for washing veggies is saved in the sink and tipped into the garden. The frugality is refreshing. It is this attitude of consuming less and reusing more that is natural for many older Chinese people. It's even more ingrained, I think, than it is in people of my parents' and grandparents' generations in Australia. Could that be because we have always had plenty? The need to save and conserve is something we could all learn.

Chinese people see the activity of growing your own food as a worthwhile pastime. Unfortunately, most people in China can't partake in it because they have no land. The last time I was in Qingdao, I found locals growing veggies underneath the big electric power line, where there was some public land. Locals had staked out small areas of soil and had started growing food. There were dozens of little farms, but my mother-in-law has since told me that it's all been pulled up. The local government had a crackdown and destroyed all the gardens, because they were against the law. The people probably knew it was prohibited, but took a chance anyway. I thought of all those people whose hard work planting and watering had been destroyed and felt sad for them, and I was grateful that we have land to garden in our backyard.

What is retirement for?

It is interesting to compare how my parents enjoy their free time as they begin their retirement to how my Chinese parents-in-law use their time. For my mother, some spare time is allocated to helping out people in the family, to spending time with my children, babysitting occasionally and doing some community work, but when the chores are done, life is all about the fun to be had: dining, exercising, lunching, going on trips, shopping, meeting friends, wining, entertaining and outings…

For my parents-in-law, however, there is no such frivolity. There are the daily tasks to be completed, including shopping, preparing food, exercising and resting. My father-in-law does dine out and drink a lot with his work colleagues, but not very often with his family. There is a great contrast between how my Mum lives and how my mother-in-law lives. Some of this is due to their different personalities, and part of it is because of the sizeable gap between their incomes for much of their lives. Although my parents-in-law do actually have the money to live a more lavish lifestyle in their retirement, they choose not to. I think that this is more to do with the Chinese perception of how one should experience life. They are living life according to the motto that personal thrift is a virtue.

Money in the Bank

The Chinese private savings rate sits at around 50%. This means that if they take home 3000 yuan a month, they save 1500 yuan. They don't save it and then spend it all in the next few months on new clothes and a holiday. They save it. Forever. In case. They save because they need cash to pay for school fees, because there is no such thing as a free education in China – all schools charge fees. If anyone in their family gets sick, they need bucket-loads of cash on hand to pay the medical fees. There is no Medicare or pharmaceutical benefits scheme in China. They need more money if someone is sick to buy presents for the doctor, so that they'll get preferential treatment. If anyone in their family crashes the car, they need cash to buy a new one, because they don't trust insurance companies so they don't insure anything. They never take out a loan to buy a car – they only buy a car if they have the cash on hand to do so. They work and save first, and then buy the trappings of an opulent lifestyle.

In the West, it is the opposite. Many people put everything on credit and take out loans and live the flashy lifestyle now. So that is how it works out that Americans are pretty much living on the savings of the Chinese people. Chinese people are increasingly borrowing to buy their houses, but a visa card in China is usually a debit card. They don't spend money till they have it.

The importance of prosperity

My mother-in-law once told me that I'd have a good life because I have large ear lobes. She also said my son will never be short of money, because in the professional photo of him we had taken when he was just three months old, he has his little fingers curled up into tight fists. She said that this means he'll hold onto his money tightly, and so will be prosperous.

In a similar vein, some Chinese people play a game with their babies when they are 100 days old. They put a lot of little things in front of their baby – some money, some food and some other toys. What the baby grabs is thought to be a sign of what they will do with their lives.

A FLYING KISS

In English, we say that we "blow kisses". In Chinese, you don't blow a kiss – you send it flying. Isn't that cute?

FAMILY FINANCES

In Chinese families, money is communal. Whatever money is earned by an individual is shared with people in their family. If the grandparents are earning more money than their children, they will help out with clothes for the grandchildren and school fees. If the grandparents are elderly and not working, the young working relatives will provide for them. There is definitely no bill-splitting at a family dinner at a restaurant – the person with the most money pays.

When my husband was young, working and still living at home, he'd bring his entire pay packet home and give it to his mum, who managed the finances. He didn't need much money to spend then (actually, he still doesn't really spend money on things for himself), but when we were going out, his mum would hand him a small pile of fresh notes to spend on me to treat me well. This is very different to Western culture, where people are expected to become financially independent when they become an adult and receive an inheritance when their parents die.

Birthday noodles

On your birthday, it is lucky to eat noodles. Long noodles. It is thought that eating very long noodles on your birthday leads to longevity. Bring on the bowl of pho or laksa or wuntun mian.

Yum.

PRIORITISING

I once attended a Chinese culture training session in Australia run by a Chinese man. It was interesting to see what he thought Aussies going to China needed to learn about Chinese people.

Here's one thing I found particularly interesting: He described a scenario in which a Western man would make a very different choice to a Chinese man. The man discovers his mother, his wife and his daughter are all drowning. Which one does he save first? A Western man saves his daughter, then his wife, then his mother.

He does so because his daughter is younger and has her whole life ahead of her, and he is responsible for her well-being. Next, he saves his wife, because he loves her and she is part of his immediate nuclear family, and she has lots of years left to live. Finally, he saves his mother.

A Chinese man saves his mother first. He owes his mother because she brought him into this world, and he cannot replace her. He can find another wife and have another child, but he can never get another mum.

This was not all that heartening to hear as the wife of a Chinese man, or as the mother of his children! But I've tried to be more understanding when my Chinese friends or family have made different choices to me, because they have their cultural reasons for doing so.

The Story of Mulan

The story of Mulan is another illustration of the way the Chinese feel they owe their parents. Mulan is a girl, but pretends to be her father to fight in a war. She does this because her father is too old to go to war, her little brother is too young, and the family is required to send one man. Mulan is a courageous warrior and fights for 10 years in her father's place. People are very surprised to eventually find out that Mulan is actually a woman. Fighting in her father's place was an amazingly brave thing to do to protect him. Disney made a movie version of Mulan in 1998, but Hua Mulan is a very old Chinese legend.

This allegiance to your parents and your family, and the sense of owing your parents everything, is very central to the Chinese belief system.

No sex education in China

Parents and schools don't routinely teach young people about sex in China. Homosexuality has only recently been legalised, and there is still much shame for a family if a young girl gets pregnant out of wedlock.

Not long after I'd met Shao Meng's parents in Qingdao, his mother turned up at his apartment early one Saturday morning. She found us having breakfast, and I was wearing little more than one of Shao Meng's t-shirts. As I heard her key turning in the lock, I cringed with the feeling of being sprung! She feigned surprise, saying: "What are you doing here?" But I think she was secretly trying to catch us having a sleepover. We just feigned innocence in response, smiling and saying the heating was better in Shao Meng's apartment, and since it was the dead of a cold Qingdao winter, I had camped down to stay warm. This seemed to appease her.

The next time I saw Shao Meng's mum, she handed me a packet of Chinese condoms, saying kindly out of concern that she wouldn't want anything to influence my job. I thanked her for her concern, and reassured her that we were being careful.

I couldn't help thinking that if his mum had taught him about sex when he was younger, she wouldn't have had to concern herself with this when her boy was approaching 30. On the other hand, there was a certain pragmatism about his mum's approach, which was refreshing. Her openness made me feel like I could discuss anything with her, and we have a fairly close relationship.

The sounds of tropical Queensland

If you stay in tropical Queensland, where my older sister resided for a while, there is a cacophony of animal sounds to wake you in the morning. Frogs, crickets and cicadas croak and chirp you off to sleep, and lots of noisy birds boisterously herald the start of a new tropical day. It really is loud, and Shao Meng couldn't believe it when he first landed in Australia.

There are not many birds at all in large Chinese cities. Good old Chairman Mao set up incentives to kill the sparrows because they ate the crops that were needed to feed the masses. And the Chinese are definitely partial to a bit of pigeon or duck – or anything with feathers, for that matter. So birds don't stand much of a chance in China. As a result, the Chinese people love to hear the bird songs here.

When she visited us a couple of years ago, my mother-in-law would get up early each morning, before 6am, to do her exercises outside on the verandah. It's during that time of morning that the birds are at their peak of noisiness. She noticed their singing and loved it. The beautiful sounds of sub-tropical wildlife can be heard even in our fairly densely populated street.

The Sounds of the Street

I had the opposite experience in China. When I first arrived in Beijing, I was living in a cosy little dormitory room that backed onto a busy street. The 375 bus would go by from early in the morning to late in the evening, and the conductor would be blasting the names of the stops through a loudspeaker on the side of the bus as it whizzed past. Big blue trucks would noisily career past. I would awaken each morning to the sound of the Beijing people commuting. This was a very new sound for me. I can still remember the sounds and the smells of that dorm room, and what a wonderfully exciting time it was for me as I embarked on getting to know a whole new culture and a whole new world.

Big breakfast

There is a well-known rhyme in Chinese about meal sizes. It says: Eat well at breakfast, eat until full at lunchtime and eat a little dinner. At breakfast, then, you can eat a lot of everything on offer. Chinese people won't eat sour things at breakfast and think it strange that we like orange juice or grapefruit in the morning. I know of some Chinese people who say they don't eat meat at breakfast.

One of my favourite big breakfasts in China is something you could buy everywhere on the streets for the meagre sum of the equivalent of 10 Aussie cents when I first went there in 1997. It consisted of a big bowl of hot, freshly-squeezed soy milk (they call it "soy juice" rather than "milk" in Chinese) with no additives except sugar and a really yummy youtiao (directly translated to mean "oily stick") – and it's like nothing you've ever had before. Youtiao is made of oily dough that puffs up when it is deep-fried in hot oil. It is made in a similar way to a doughnut, but it tastes very different – it is not sweet or squishy. It is very greasy and crunchy, and served hot. Some Chinese people dip the youtiao in the soy milk.

The next breakfast course follows (I told you breakfast was big). This is a bowl of won ton (which is actually "huntun" in Mandarin) soup. The final course is baozi – little round dumplings made with wheat flour with pork inside. Oh yes – this is the kind of food that makes me miss China. But this kind of street breakfast is harder to find in flash, fancy Beijing and even in Qingdao, it is only found in little local streets. When we stayed in Qingdao the last couple of times, my father-in-law went out to buy the youtiao for breakfast on his days off. Oh, they were so good!

As the next part of the saying goes, at lunchtime you should eat until full. I love canteen lunches in China. As a worker, every lunchtime you can always find a canteen that caters for office employees. There is usually some kind of card system where you purchase your lunch passes in advance, or if you are lucky, your employer gives them to you. This could be a remnant from the pure communist days. The free lunch is not very common though, because some people wasted the food if they got it for free, so most employers make their staff pay a small fee. The food is good and fresh, and the portions are generous. It is usually served on a stainless steel platter. You line up and file past a production line of people serving, where someone gives you a big pile of rice. You can then choose from a few dishes – usually a meat, a fish, a tofu dish, maybe an egg dish, and usually a few different kinds of individual vegetables. There is often also a soup, which is usually a clear broth.

In Northern Chinese cooking, they don't throw veggies in with the meat dishes, or mix different kinds of vegetables in one dish. Vegetables are usually very fresh and cooked on their own in a hot wok, with lots of oil and salt (and maybe garlic), and taste very good (I'm thinking about eggplant or English spinach as I write).

One of the disadvantages of the canteen lunch is that you have to eat on time or it is cold, or the canteen is closed. If a meeting goes over and you miss the canteen, then you have to make extra effort to find food. As a result, meetings usually finish just in time for lunch. Employers of large numbers of people find having a big canteen on site pays off, because people don't go home to eat (which was common a couple of decades ago, when workers went home for two hours between 12pm and 2pm to cook a hot lunch and have a sleep). Some people still do this in some parts of China – it's very civilised and another example of slow living, but it does tend to cut into your workday. If workers don't have to leave the factory or office for lunch, it saves time, and the bosses can get more out of their workers. I liked it because I never had to make my lunch and I didn't have to spend a fortune on a bought lunch. And it sure beats sandwiches!

Then for dinner, you are supposed to eat just a little meal. It occurs to me that this is often the spiel you hear from nutritionists in the West. They suggest that it is better to have a big breakfast and a small dinner, so you do not go to bed with a full stomach. So the Chinese who eat according to this rhyme are usually fit and healthy.

Where are all the people?

I've spoken to lots of Chinese visitors to Australia (and I've read this in books by Chinese people on their first impressions of Australian cities, too) who say the first thing they wondered when they arrived was: where are all the people? They saw lots of houses and lots of cars, but no people. In China, there are houses and cars, but also people absolutely everywhere. They usually also notice our big, beautiful old trees and our lovely green grass, and if it is fine, our beautiful blue sky with fluffy white clouds drifting across it.

I had an English friend in Beijing when I was first there, during which time the smog was impenetrable, and I remember her remarking to me once: "The thing I miss most about London is the different skies – the patterns the clouds make, the different colours of a sunset." On another occasion, she said how sad she was because the sun had been reduced to a tiny orange thing trying to shine through layers of dust and smog. I could count on my hands the number of days in 1997 when we had blue skies in Beijing. We were overjoyed and astonished to see mountain ranges in the distance one day when the sky was blue. We'd been living in Beijing for months before we saw these.

For a newly-arrived Chinese, on the other hand, the suburbs of Australia can feel like a very desolate ghost town. My husband has often said that he feels good when he hears someone in our neighbourhood having a rowdy party or a shouting match. It is comforting for him to hear that there is life in the suburbs. It makes him realise that there are people nearby after all.

Morbid fascination

Have you noticed that whenever there is a car accident, the resultant traffic jam is worsened by drivers who experience morbid fascination and slow down so they can have a good look at what happened? In China, you can multiply this by an intensity factor of about 10. Add in the huge population, and you soon have a massive crowd gathering to watch whatever dramatic event is happening. If there is an altercation on the street or an accident, then everybody stops to look – not to help or to give first aid, but to look. They form a huge crowd around the injured person so they can watch what is happening. The stranger's plight is of great interest. If they tried to help, they might be blamed for something, or they worry that they might get roped into paying the ambulance or hospital fees. I've heard of foreigners pushing their way in to give first aid even when they don't speak Chinese, while lots of locals watch on.

Foreigners on TV

We have satellite TV at our house, and we've got the dish pointed to the Chinese TV satellite, so we have about 50 free Chinese channels. Shao Meng, like most blokes, likes to zone out in front of the box after a day at the office or on the weekend. I thought if it is going to be chattering away, it may as well be chattering away in Chinese – a bit of learning by osmosis for the kids. He flicks channels all the time, so you get a good sample of what's on. Not a day goes by without some show containing footage of a foreigner living in China and speaking Chinese. Chinese people are fascinated by foreigners speaking Chinese. If the foreigner speaks well, they are really impressed; if the foreigner speaks badly, they find it endearing. I find this strange. Imagine if we in Australia invited a selection of people new to Australia onto TV and had them speak English, just for our amusement?

When I went to China for the third time in 2001, a few weeks in, my Australian classmates and I were offered money to go on a variety show on TV. They had us speak Chinese and taste rotten tofu (a kind of equivalent to our blue cheese). They thought this was funny. About six months later, I was buying chewing gum at a little convenience store and the shopkeeper recognised me from the show. That was even weirder – I was known because I had been seen on TV as a Chinese-speaking foreigner. How many Chinese people are there in Australia who are famous because they speak English?

"WANG RHYMES WITH TONGUE"

That's what I tell my children's teachers. My husband and children's last name is Wang, but I didn't change my name to Wang when we were married because I would feel weird having a Chinese last name when I am not Chinese. Also, Chinese women don't change their names when they get married – they have the same name their whole life. Shao Meng neither wanted nor expected me to change my name. My Dad, though, thought it was a bit weird that I was keeping my surname after I was married.

Just as Smith, Jones and Brown are common English surnames, Wang, Li, Liu and Zhang are common Chinese surnames. Most people have got the pronunciation of Li right. When referring to Li Na (surname Li, first name Na), the famous tennis player, the media now know that Li is pronounced as "Lee" rather than "Lie". But everyone in Australia seems to struggle with the rest of these common Chinese surnames. Wang does not rhyme with "gang". The "a" sound is the long vowel sound as in "castle" or "dance", so it rhymes with "tongue". Generally when Aussies say Wang, it sounds terrible and I cringe. So now you know: "Wang rhymes with tongue." Zhang also rhymes with "tongue", and the "zh" sound is like the "j" sound in "jug".

Lucy Liu, the famous Chinese actor, has a common last name but it is often pronounced incorrectly as "Loo". It is actually pronounced "Leeo", with an accent on the "lee" sound.

Babies crawling on the wedding bed

Here's a lovely Chinese wedding tradition: The night before the wedding, the family arranges for someone's baby son to come play and crawl on the wedding bed, to bring good fortune to the newlyweds so that they may have lots of children.

We had planned for such an event in Qingdao the night before our wedding, but the baby boy got stuck in traffic. I was very distraught, because I liked the sound of this tradition, and I thought time was running out. So I rang my colleague Steven, whose wife had recently had a bouncing baby girl (and this was a very cute baby). He and his wife did the honours, and brought the beautiful smiley baby girl to crawl on our beautifully-made red wedding bed. My husband spoiled it for me, though: after they left, he said it wasn't quite right because it was supposed to have been a boy baby. I reminded him through gritted teeth of the Chinese propaganda slogan – boys and girls are the same. Chinese preference for boy babies is very deeply ingrained.

Feng shui

My understanding of feng shui is that your local environment in and around your home needs to be taken into account. The word "feng" means "wind" and "shui" means "water". Many factors, like how the weather affects the home and its position in relation to other elements of the surrounding landscape (like mountains and rivers or oceans), are all conceived to affect feng shui. Improving the feng shui of your home improves its liveability and means that you are more likely to live a long and prosperous life there.

I learnt a lot about feng shui when my husband and I bought our house in Brisbane. We looked at lots and lots of houses during our search for the right one. I'd be looking at the size of the kitchen benches and how cute it looked and whether or not the house needed more renovating. Shao Meng would shake his head and say: "Oh no, the driveway is sloping the wrong way – all our money will flow out." Or: "There are too many angles pointing to our house, we can't live on a corner like this." The house we ended up buying was one he thought had great feng shui. It does seem to be bringing us lots of gifts: we have three healthy children here, after all. When he sees birds making their nests in a tree in our yard, he comments on the good feng shui – even the birds feel it.

Super mum

My mother-in-law said I was lihai (translated to mean "amazing", in a favourable way) when she saw me doing the grocery shopping. She said I was doing things that no modern-day Chinese mother would do. After the birth of my third child, when my parents-in-law were staying with us, I took a good month to relax with my new baby girl and recover. When the month was over, I was very keen to go about doing my usual tasks. Grocery shopping is, of course, one of them. I don't like it, but I try to do a fairly sizeable shop on a regular basis so that we have enough for about a week.

On this particular day, I took all three kids in the car. I put the baby in the baby carrier, my toddler in the trolley and my preschool son walked alongside as I filled the trolley. Then I loaded the groceries into the car with the kids and drove home. It took about an hour and a half. My mother-in-law was amazed and praised me for a good hour afterwards. She remarked that I just do the work and I don't complain, whereas young Chinese women today would not be up to it. They get tired. They go out shopping for clothes and leave the parents to do the food shopping.

I actually think we are pretty lucky – at least I can drive the car and don't have to take public transport. Also, Chinese women would mostly go back to work full-time when the children are a few months old, to earn money. They lead a life not that dissimilar to their life before children. Grandparents do the childrearing and housework. Both the money and the childrearing tasks are shared. I don't feel hard done by, staying at home and working unpaid to raise my kids and take care of the household tasks. I enjoy it. I don't want to hand my kids over to their grandparents every day. I am giving up career time and leisure time, but I do so willingly. My mother-in-law was implying that she was very grateful that I was working so hard to raise her grandchildren.

Parents and children living apart

I know of two Chinese families here in Brisbane in which the parents have been separated from their very young child for an extended period. In one case, when the child was an infant and required 24-hour care, the parents wanted to keep working, so they left their child in China while they both worked on building their own business here in Australia. In the other case, the parents left their child in Australia with the grandparents while they went to China to work. I feel very sad when I hear these stories. I experience a physical pain myself when I think about it, and I feel anxiety. I am always so happy to see my kids after they have been babysat while I've been out to dinner for just a few hours.

I wonder about how the mothers cope with the long physical separation from the child they gave birth to. How can they function at work? I don't understand how the longing doesn't take over all their thoughts. I also wonder about the effect it would have on the child's psyche. Will the sense of abandonment affect their emotional development? I think it has to sever, to some extent, that intimate bond between mother and child and father and child.

I wonder whether this practice of separating mothers and babies will fade out as China's standard of living improves. Or perhaps it is characteristic of the non-nuclear family structure, with the wider family caring for each other – so long as someone is doing it, it doesn't have to be the mother who raises the child.

And Husbands and Wives, Too

I was having a manicure in Qingdao one day and was chatting to the woman next to me. Her husband was working in the United States and was not able to return home, possibly because of visa issues. They had a son who was 11 years old, and the husband sent money home for them. I thought that was fair enough. I asked her when he was coming home next, and she said she didn't know. I then asked when he'd come home to visit last, and she replied that he hadn't at all. He'd been there seven years; his son was four when he left, and now was 11. Seven years away from his family! I felt so sad for this woman, and then I wondered if maybe she liked it this way. Maybe her husband had a new family in the US now, and he was keeping two wives. How would I know? How would she know, come to think of it?

Shao Meng has a friend who is a doctor at a hospital. His wife is also well educated, and went to Europe for two years to do her master's degree. This kind of marital separation while staying married seems to happen often in China. Not my cup of tea! I figure you get married to be together, so the least you can do is live in the same place.

Simplified characters

Mao Zedong changed the written Chinese language to increase literacy rates. The Chinese written language has hundreds of thousands of characters. The characters consist of different elements: some have a phonetic component, which tell you how it is pronounced; some have a meaning component; and some have neither, so you just have to guess.

To help people learn the written language, Mao Zedong took approximately 2,000 characters and simplified them, so that it was faster and easier to learn to read and write. This really helped, and more people became literate. That's why you hear people talking about simplified characters and traditional characters.

In Taiwan and Hong Kong, only traditional characters are in use.

Wrinkles

Lots of Chinese people come to Australia, and when they feel comfortable enough to be candid about what they've observed, they will tell you that they notice the number of overweight people in Australia. They also notice the wrinkles. Chinese skin seems to stand up to the ravages of the sun better than Anglo skin. In addition, the strong Aussie sun beats down and many people do not apply sunscreen daily. Some people also routinely sunbathed in the past. This all contributes to giving people wrinkles.

Conversely, I often admire the smooth, wrinkle-free skin of the Chinese people I meet. They are always vigilant with their sun protection. They wear hats, long sleeves on hot days, and driving gloves to keep their hands out of the sun's rays when they are driving in Australia. If they are caught somewhere without sun protection, they will grab whatever they can to shade their face for fear of getting a tan or wrinkles.

DR PHIL

My husband's eyes and ears popped out of his head when he turned on daytime television in Australia to find American people airing their family's dirty linen on TV. He could not understand why a couple would want to bring their pregnant, unwed teenage daughter on stage for all the world to see. A Chinese family would try to avoid the shame and would hide her away to prevent bringing their family into disrepute. The idea that going on TV and broadcasting your problems would be a step towards solving your family's issues is incomprehensible. This was a major culture shock for Shao Meng. Chinese people don't really go for psychological therapy, because they don't like sharing their problems with a stranger. They are more likely to seek family involvement to resolve relationship problems that meet an impasse. Seeking psychological therapy in front of the whole world is very hard for them to fathom.

Everybody gives way to everybody

Here is a genuine road safety rule of thumb promoted in Qingdao. It is called San Rang, which means "three give-ways": cars give way to other cars; cars give way to pedestrians; pedestrians give way to cars. Not only does the government promote this in Qingdao, they also hold Qingdao up as a glowing example of traffic compliance across other regions of China. While I agree that Qingdao's traffic is fairly orderly compared to other Chinese cities and the blowing of horns is not as common, I'm not sure how you are supposed to figure out who is giving way to whom. It tends to happen like this: I move a little to see if you are going to move, and if you are, then I stop and let you go. This is seriously how it works. Can it work any other way when the three give-ways are in force?

Chinese Frére Jacques

"Frére Jacques" turns out to be a universal nursery rhyme. It was originally composed in French, and there is also an English version. In China, they use the same tune, but they aren't singing about Brother John. The song is about two tigers, one with no ears and one without a tail.

According to the song, the two tigers are running very quickly. The final line is: "really strange". I was singing the Chinese version of this nursery rhyme to my daughter and her kindergarten class, and as I was explaining the meaning, it didn't seem right. It felt as though we were pointing out the tigers' disabilities and then saying how really strange they were, and it didn't sit right with me. One of my daughter's teachers, Christine, quickly pointed out that we love them anyway, which was a beautiful way of saying to the children that it doesn't matter what you are missing, you are still worthy of love and you are not strange at all.

For me, this is a good way of pointing out how the Chinese don't show much political correctness when it comes to disabilities. They are known to stare in fascination at anyone different, even if your only difference is that you have different coloured skin. A couple of African American friends in Beijing said they often had trouble hailing a cab because of racism against black people.

There are no public amenities for wheelchairs, and no ramps or lifts in many buildings. The pavements are very uneven. You rarely see people with disabilities on the streets because many of them have been moved away to live in special homes, or they are kept at home to be cared for. There is a shame associated with people with disabilities.

I am sure that with modernisation and better education levels, this is improving. And I am hopeful that this is the case.

Wade & Giles, tones and Cantonese

Do you want to know why Beijing used to be called Peking, and why Canton is now referred to as Guangdong (the province closest to Hong Kong)? Or why Mao Tze-Tung is now Mao Zedong?

First there was the Wade Giles system. Then when pinyin was introduced, the Wade Giles system became obsolete. But some of the old Wade Giles spelling conventions have hung on.

A long time ago, two blokes called Wade and Giles came up with a method for writing Chinese in Roman letters. Their way is not used much any more – pinyin is now the official method. Pinyin is the name for the official Romanisation of Mandarin. This means that if you want to write Chinese in Roman letters without using characters, then you use pinyin.

As well as using "abc" letters to spell out Chinese words, pinyin uses lines on top of the words to represent the tone of the word. Mandarin has four tones: the first tone is high and of level pitch; the second is a rising tone, going from low to high quite quickly; the third tone is a dipping pitch that starts high, dips and goes up again; and the fourth tone is a sharp falling tone. It sounds confusing, eh? It's not as confusing as Cantonese, which has nine tones. Did you ever wonder why you can never really find a course to learn Cantonese? That's because they don't exist – you can't study Cantonese at university. You are either born into a family that uses the language, or you are not.

If you are learning Chinese, you need to learn pinyin, because if you hear someone say a word and you don't know what it means, you need to know how to spell it in pinyin to be able to look it up. Pinyin is one way of typing in Chinese. So for example, if you wanted to type "Beijing" into your computer, you would type the letters "b-e-i-j-i-n-g" and it will guess the characters of Beijing, and you can just select it. This actually makes it much easier for me, as I can recognise a lot more characters than I can remember how to write. Consequently, I can write better in Chinese on a computer than I can with a pen and paper. Hooray for technology!

Conclusion: May the sampling continue

It is difficult to say: "That's it… that's everything I know as a member of a modern Chinese family, and that's everything I've observed about Chinese people over the years." As I said, there are many layers to the Chinese way of life to uncover. It's fun and I'm excited about learning more. I know I'll have more to write about in the future, but this is my first offering.

If you'd like to share some of your insights, I'd love to hear which of the "dumplings" in this book resonate with you on your China journey. In the meantime, I hope I've whet your appetite further, and that you'll continue to read and delve into the history, language, philosophy and culture of China.

Acknowledgements

Thanks to my lovely family, friends, clients and teachers. Thanks especially to my Mum and sisters for reading lots of early versions and proofreading this book, and for their insightful comments.

I would also like to thank Jenna Barlow for being my editor, and Linda Diggle for helping me to publish the book.

www.ingramcontent.com/pod-product-compliance
Lightning Source LLC
Chambersburg PA
CBHW072058290426
44110CB00014B/1739